CAREERS IN

CW00523484

ARCHITECTURE

CAREERS IN

ARCHITECTURE

Oliver Burston

fifth edition

KOGAN
PAGE

Acknowledgements

The author would like to thank the staff of the Royal Institute of British Architects and many others for their help in compiling this book.

First published in 1982
Second edition 1989
Third edition 1993
Fourth edition 1995
Fifth edition 1997

Kogan Page Limited
120 Pentonville Road
London N1 9JN

© Kogan Page 1982, 1989, 1993, 1995, 1997

British Library Cataloguing in Publication Data

A CIP record for this book is available from the British Library.

ISBN 0 7494 2384 6

Typeset by Kogan Page Ltd
Printed and bound in Great Britain by Clays Ltd, St Ives plc

Contents

Introduction

Is this the Job for You?

- ☐ Are you good at analysing abstract problems?

- ☐ An architect's unique skill is the ability to visualise a three-dimensional concept of a building which solves the abstract problems he has analysed.

- ☐ If you are able to draw, paint, sculpt, take good photographs or produce videos you are more likely to have the visual ability required. Freehand sketches, presentation drawings, hand-drawn architectural drawings and computer aided architectural drawings are all skills you will need to acquire.

- ☐ A thorough knowledge of building construction is essential. If you are good at making or repairing things you are likely to have a natural feel for construction.

- ☐ Being naturally observant is helpful when making site inspections and checking drawings.

- ☐ The practice of architecture involves a lot of letter writing, reports and the administrative side of running building contracts.

- ☐ You must be able to get on with people. Buildings are designed by teams of architects operating within a wider team which includes other building professionals such as engineers. You must be able to develop a close rapport with your clients, building contractors and inspectors such as the building control inspector.

❑ To find clients you will need to develop contacts. Are you likeable or sociable?

❑ Architectural practices are businesses. Public sector departments are also increasingly run on business lines. Can you work under pressure?

❑ Would you be comfortable with an irregular stream of work? Building is project-oriented and when the project is finished you need to find another. Architectural services are increasingly procured for part of the building process only, making projects shorter, and architects often have to put in a lot of work with only a small chance of getting a paid commission.

❑ As a professional you need to demonstrate a high level of fairness and integrity.

❑ All the activities of architectural practice are very time-consuming so you must be prepared to work hard, both as a student and as a practising architect.

❑ The financial rewards of architecture can be poor and are not improving, so make sure that becoming an architect is what you really want to do.

❑ You need GCSEs and A-levels to study architecture, and preferably a mix of science and arts subjects.

What is an architect?

Shelter, like food and water, is a fundamental need of human beings. We all need shelter from the elements, fierce sun, pouring rain, howling wind. We also need security, although its nature changes according to the society in which we live; for example, brick houses would not stop nuclear missiles but they can stop burglars. We also value privacy.

In simple, so-called primitive societies, the same person is client, architect and builder. As society becomes more complex, a greater proportion of buildings are erected by builders.

The architect*

But who decides what the builder should build? Even today the vast majority of the world's buildings are built according to customs and traditions. These change sufficiently slowly for the builders to know what they are expected to build, and the clients to know what they are getting without the need for a designer or architect who will produce designs, generally in the form of drawings and models for his client's approval, and then working drawings to tell the builders how and what to build.

However, as society, and the buildings that society requires, become more complex a separate occupation of building designer, or architect, comes into being. In Britain today most new building is designed by architects, and much of all building work is handled by architects or other 'professionals'.

The description given above is a simplification of what actually happened at different periods and in different parts of the world, and is given in order to illustrate how the role of the architect fits into the overall process of commissioning, designing and constructing a building. It should be emphasised, however, that the roots of both building and architecture go back far beyond written records, to a time when there was no division in people's minds between art, science, philosophy or religion and no concepts of professionals, civil servants or business men as we know them. Therefore it is not surprising that architects cannot be conveniently labelled as 'artists', 'scientists' or 'professionals' because they must be all three.

Allied professions

As buildings, along with society as a whole, have become more complex, building designers have specialised in different areas and totally separate professions have grown up. Indeed the

---

* Please note that the male pronoun has been used throughout this book to refer to both male and female architects.

surveyor has probably been around as long as the architect – in the sixteenth century the terms were synonymous.

Today there are many types of surveyor: for example, the quantity surveyor who specialises in preparing bills of quantities and in advising how much a building will cost; and the building surveyor whose skills overlap those of the architect to a considerable extent, particularly when dealing with repair work to existing buildings. Separate professional disciplines also exist for structural engineers, electrical engineers and mechanical engineers – the latter dealing with the services needed to provide heating, ventilating and water services to a building.

There is also a separate profession of technicians who act in a supportive role to the architect, particularly in carrying out drawings and technical details. Interior designers specialise in the internal appearance of buildings, landscape architects in landscaping and planting; industrial designers design, among other things, furniture, equipment and fittings which go into buildings; town planners deal with the design of towns and the operation of the planning laws and regulations.

Many of the original members of some of these professions were architects, and some architects today hold dual qualifications. On the other hand, most architects specialise in one or two areas of work. The commonest division is into building types, such as hospitals, housing or theatres. An alternative, much more common in the United States, is division into different aspects of the design process, that is to say design concept, information for the builder, supervision of construction. Some architects also offer specialist advice, for example on building failures or making architectural models. Others specialise in teaching, writing and journalism. Further specialisms also exist for architects and other building professionals such as in lighting or acoustics, and there are new spheres such as energy assessment and computer aided design.

In short, the architect combines the roles of designer of three-dimensional space, construction design and project management, but his unique skill is his ability to visualise a building in three dimensions and produce a conceptual design for it.

Case Study

Julian *has his own practice in north London.*

'When I left school I got a job at the Architectural Association taking technical photographs and looking after equipment for the building technology lecturers. I already had a place at the Architectural Association School of Architecture which I took up the following year.

After Part 1, I went to Sri Lanka for a year under a Voluntary Service Overseas scheme. I worked for a UNESCO-sponsored organisation which was carrying out research into school building in that part of the world. I returned to the AA and completed Part 2.

After getting my diploma I was offered a job with GMW Architects but was employed on the detailed planning of a large hospital project and found I was not getting the experience necessary to pass Part 3 (Professional Practice). After six months I left and joined a small practice. I got experience of lots of different small projects, did working drawings and quickly saw them being built and had my own small projects to design and manage on site.

Shortly after passing Part 3, I got married and bought a house. I had a heavy mortgage and needed a job that paid better, so I got a job with SEF Architects as project architect for a large public housing scheme for the GLC in Westminster. This was my first experience of the adversarial world of large contracting and again was very good experience working directly for an experienced associate.

However, work was drying up, and I was offered a job with the London Borough of Islington Architects Department in a group designing buildings for the social services. I designed a hostel for adults with learning difficulties, but unfortunately the long decline in public sector projects had begun and the scheme was not built. However I designed a block of flats, originally part of the same site, which was built. On the strength of this I was asked to join a new group which was being set up to survey and renovate Islington's old and decaying estates. This was a chance to put into practice many of the ideas on housing that I had learnt at college ten years before – such as involving the residents in the design of their new flats.

I stayed at Islington for ten years but was increasingly restless and wanted to return to the private sector. This I did and spent the next ten years as an associate in two central London firms specialising in public sector housing. When I was at Islington, I had developed interests in computers in architecture, and energy assessment. The flexible working hours at Islington had enabled me to do courses on both subjects. In the 1980s CAD and energy assessment were at the experimental stage.

However, in the 1990s most offices invested in CAD and I became CAD manager. I also opened my own energy assessment consultancy and initially I took a day a week off to build up my own practice. After I had been doing that for a year, I was made redundant. Fortunately, this was at a time when the building industry was starting to pick up after the longest and deepest recession since the war and I found that both consultancy work (I added Planning Supervisor work under Health and Safety Regulations) and architectural commissions started to pick up. When I hit a slow patch, I also help out other practices.

I have now been in full-time practice for about 18 months and I am enjoying the freedom of working for myself. My aim is to expand at about 50 per cent a year and, with a full year behind me, that looks a realistic objective provided we do not have another slump. Most of the projects I have at the moment are one-off house renovations, but I have done feasibility studies for much larger projects and I hope that next year one or more of these will become a reality.'

---

2 What does an architect do?

Introduction

Although an architect's job may involve one or more of a large range of tasks, some of which are only remotely related to the design and construction of buildings, the central role of an architect is that of project architect.

Essentially, the project architect carries out three tasks: conceptual design, construction design and project management. These correspond to the three main stages of a building project, which are design concept, information for the builder and site supervision.

The design concept comes together in the architect's mind as a result of the information he has absorbed about the building requirements and the site characteristics. The design concept is usually communicated to the client and to other members of the design team by drawings and models. The building requirements consist of a diverse and often conflicting collection of planning and environmental factors. Some of these will be readily available from books and other publications, or from the architect's previous experience; others will involve research.

Site analysis consists of factors such as aesthetic relationship to other buildings, orientation, existing features on the site, bearing capacity of the ground, and location of underground services.

The architect also has to take into account such constraints as cost, building life, construction time, statutory requirements (planning permission/building control/drainage approval/ means of escape approval), structure, construction and services.

Conceptual design

The design concept is initially very diagrammatic, but as each part of the building is worked out in greater detail it is translated into a building design. The drawings which an architect produces consist of plans, sections, elevations and projections. Projections are an attempt to portray the three-dimensional nature of a building and consist of perspectives and metric projections. Metric projections are methods of drawing buildings or objects so as to give an impression of actual three-dimensional appearance in such a way as to allow length, breadth and height to be measured. The most commonly used projections are axonometric and isometric.

Nowadays most drawings are produced on computer using computer aided design (CAD) software. This not only speeds up the process of drawing, but allows much more sophisticated views, including walk-through presentations which give the effect of being inside the building.

Architects generally work in design teams. These consist of architects, surveyors and engineers. They work for a client who is the person or public body that has commissioned the building.

Detail design

Producing production information, from which the builder builds the building, is the most time-consuming stage of a new building project. This is recognised by the RIBA fee scale, which apportions 40 per cent of the total fee for this stage. Although the primary purpose of production information is to explain to the builder how to build the building, the drawings are first sent to the quantity surveyor so that he can measure the amount of each different building operation.

The drawings, and bills of quantities (as the document produced by the quantity surveyor is called), are then sent to a number of builders to produce a tender, in other words to price to see who will do the job cheapest. The procedure is in fact rigorously controlled. In addition to the information about the building sent to the builder describing in detail the location, details and specification of each element, a precise time is given when all information is simultaneously sent out to each builder about how long he has to complete his tender and when all tenders will be opened. Normally the lowest tender is accepted.

Production drawings are also sent to the various statutory authorities for their approval, except for the planning authority which is sent design drawings at a much earlier stage in the project.

The precise amount and format of the information varies. In general large projects are detailed and documented to a much greater extent than small ones; these may consist of a specification rather than the more elaborate bills of quantities, and relatively few drawings. However, the architect is responsible for the detail design of a building unless it is a 'design and build' contract when the architect does the design and the builder produces the details. More unqualified and inexperienced staff are employed at this stage than any other owing to the large amount of draughting and because there is a high proportion of routine work as opposed to key decision making.

In carrying out production information, the architect normally has the expert assistance of not only the quantity surveyor who produces the bills of quantities but also various engineers, such as the structural engineers who produce their own drawings and specifications. However, on one subject – the construction – the architect normally has no specialist adviser, so it is important to realise that in addition to being the conceptual designer, the architect must be the construction expert. Moreover, this is a skill which can only be satisfactorily acquired in practice.

Project management

Many people might think that once a builder – normally the one who puts in the lowest price – is appointed, the architect's job is done. However, the traditional method in this country is for the architect to take on the role of project manager and administrator of the contract between the building procurer and the contractor.

The clerk of works is the client's representative on site and, together with the architect, is responsible for seeing that the work is carried out in conformity with the drawings and specification. On large jobs there will also be specialist inspectors, for example for the electrical and mechanical installations.

Site supervision is particularly onerous on work to existing buildings. This is largely because the full extent of repairs cannot be finalised until the fittings, decorations and, for example, plaster have been removed. Therefore the architect has to produce further information in the form of schedules and drawings, being careful to keep to a strict timetable to avoid delaying the builder and thus causing his client expense.

However, the majority of the tasks which an architect does at this stage are of an administrative nature in his role as project coordinator. These include client liaison, monitoring cost control, evaluation of tenders, chairing regular site progress meetings, dealing with claims from the builder for extensions to the contract period and increased costs, arranging the hand-over of the site to the builder, checking the work near completion to see that it is to the required standard, arranging the handing back of the site to the client, inspecting the building at the end of the defects liability period, and issuing regular certificates which the builder presents to the client for payment of work done.

At the same time he continues to coordinate the design team, and any variations – whether architect's or specialist's drawings – are issued to the builder through the architect on what is known as architect's instructions. He also has to sort out any problems with the building inspector and deal with any problems from adjoining owners.

Design and build

Various types of design and build contract are gaining in popularity at the expense of the traditional contract. The main reason for this is that the building procurer feels that he thus knows at the start of a project what the final cost will be. With design and build contracts there is usually an employer's agent. Sometimes he is an architect, but more often he is a quantity surveyor.

There are a number of types of design and build contract. For example, the building procurer may commission an architect to design the building, and a quantity surveyor to produce the written tender documents. The quantity surveyor may remain the employer's agent and the architect be nominated to produce the working drawings but work directly for the contractor.

Another type of design and build is when the contractor commissions the architect to produce a design. As several contractors normally tender in competition, this means that several different architects will each produce a design and in many cases only the architect working for the successful contractor will get paid for the work he has done.

Case Study

Andy is working in a private practice office in the North of England, prior to taking Part 3.

'When I started off here I got a little design of some fishing chalets to do. I think it was just to test me. Unfortunately it did not go ahead. I went out on site but the problem at the time was that there was not much work in the office. There were a couple of jobs that I got involved with just as a draughtsman. Most jobs were either at design stage or they were on site. I tended to go round and see how other folk in the office were getting on and go out to see different jobs on site, taking minutes at site meetings etc, just to get out of the office. If you sit around all day you are not going to get anyone coming to you and giving you experience, you have to go and look for it. I also did a fair amount of production information, and helped a lad with the design of a housing scheme for Middlesbrough, for which we ended up building a big presentation model.

When I came back here after finals I was worried they would still treat me as an intermediate student. However, at my interview I made it painfully obvious that I needed practical training to enable me to pass Part 3 and they have been pretty good that way. When I first came back into the office I did two competitions with one of the associates; the first was a housing competition, the other a limited competition for a hospice. It was quite fun doing them, coming straight from college, but the problem was that at college you are your own master, in terms of how you want to design. I found it very difficult – especially in a competition – to design for my boss. On the hospice I did most of the design, but it was changed right at the last minute with my boss coming back from holiday and we did not win. I wanted to do the hospice in a totally different idiom from the designs that the office produces, which created a bit of a problem, but it was quite an interesting experience.

I then started helping one of the associates with a couple of jobs, finishing off some production information for housing association work consisting of 16 new houses on a station site right in the town centre. We are still working on a scheme for which I did a lot of the drawings for client approval, which is a small group of seven or eight houses.

I also have a small job of my own, the conversion of a vicarage to a parish centre. The associate had done the initial feasibility study, and I took it on from there. I had client contact with someone from the building society, and the partner and associate went to the church meetings. I did not find this frustrating, however, as I was also dealing direct with the client. It is the cottages and stables attached to the old vicarage that I am converting, so we created a meeting room downstairs and put in kitchens, and then upstairs other meeting rooms. It is a really nice little job to do, because I have had to do non-standard details like bay windows to match existing, and it has gone to site quite recently, within six months of starting the design.

We had a quantity surveyor for the vicarage job, a structural engineer, but no service engineers. Working with the QS has been quite helpful; we work quite closely together. I explained to him it was the first job I had done, and I am actually going to write a case study on him for my log book for RIBA Part 3.

This year I feel that I have been taking a lot of responsibility and not being paid for it, but I think that is just a general thing in private practice. I am learning fast, but I often feel very frustrated at my lack of building knowledge. University does not teach you how to erect buildings, and not very much of what you learn at college is relevant to practice, but what you do at college lets you progress, and there is no way I could handle the things I do now without those things I did at college.'

3 The structure of the industry

The changing role of the architect

There is little record of the working lives or even the names of architects until the sixteenth century. There were architects in Classical Greece and in the Middle Ages. The traditional view is that they were master masons or sculptors, but in the absence of written records it is very dangerous to generalise as to how numerous they were or as to their precise role and status. Certainly the complexity and sophistication of the great buildings of classical and mediaeval times would have required a person or persons acting in an intermediary role between client and builder, whether he was a master mason/architect, a scholar/cleric/architect, or an independent consulting architect like his modern counterpart.

However, what is certain is that the role of the architect – be he called 'architect' or by any other name – changes with the society around him. In the period between the sixteenth and early nineteenth centuries most buildings were commissioned by the ruling classes or by wealthy institutions – church, state or otherwise – run by royalty, the aristocracy and the gentry. The men to whom these people turned when they wanted buildings designed were people they could trust and admire, and who were themselves scholars and gentlemen. Men such as Inigo Jones, Wren or Vanbrugh were as interested in astronomy or writing plays as in architecture. Renaissance and post-Renaissance scholars believed it was important to be interested in a great variety of different subjects, and this included classical architecture. Thus many of the great architects of this period came to the practice of architecture relatively late in life. Buildings were still simple enough and construction techniques sufficiently traditional for the architect not to need as much knowledge of the technical details as he does today.

The Industrial Revolution

The Industrial Revolution brought sweeping changes. There was a great increase in industrial development and in the rate at which society and technology were changing. There was also a population explosion and a migration to the towns. This provided a great need for new building, and produced a large middle class of businessmen and professionals, politicians and administrators. It was also a society with a strong belief in free enterprise and without the plethora of controls which today regulate everything from the characteristics of a brick to the required thermal insulation of a wall. Thus the Victorian architect needed to be a 'professional' who was of similar social status to his clients, whose training gave him the required technical expertise, and who could be relied on to give independent advice – in other words not to be in the pocket of an unscrupulous builder or material supplier.

The vehicle for this was a code of conduct whereby in return for giving up certain rights enjoyed by the ordinary citizen – most importantly the right to carry on his business as a limited company, to have direct links with builders such as being a director of a building company, and to advertise his services – he gained certain privileges, particularly the right to charge his fees according to a scale determined by his professional institute, to prevent other architects from competing for his clients and to restrict the right of entry to the profession to those who had passed exams set by the institute.

Although the Royal Institute of British Architects (RIBA) was founded in 1834, statutory registration of architects, and thus the enforcement of a code of conduct, was not mandatory until the

Architects Registration Act 1938. This provided that a person may not call himself an architect unless he is registered with the Architects Registration Board (ARB) (formerly the Architects Registration Council of the United Kingdom (ARCUK)), and all architects must conform with the ARB code of conduct. Unlike doctors, for example, architects do not have a monopoly of doing a particular type of work. It is not essential to be an architect to submit plans for planning permission whereas one does need to be a doctor to sign a death certificate. But if somebody calls himself an architect the public knows he has a certain minimum standard of training.

The post-second world war period

The end of the second world war brought great changes. The devastation of the war, combined with the rise of the welfare state, brought a large increase in the amount of work, particularly for government, and a large increase in the number of architects working for government, particularly for local authorities. It was also a time of heady optimism with the fusion of welfare state politics and the modern movement in architecture leading to a belief that a new, better-designed environment would solve social as well as environmental problems.

The large majority of architects were now salaried employees rather than principals or partners and this, for some, reduced the importance of professional status. This was due partly to the increasing numbers of architects in the public sector and in large private sector offices; also, the introduction of student grants made it possible for a much wider section of the population to undertake a college education. Before the war the architectural profession, like many other jobs, was to a considerable extent restricted to those whose parents could afford to pay for their training. Thus, although the vast majority of architects (80 per cent) continue to belong to the RIBA, many, particularly those in the public sector, are also trade union members.

Trade unions

The RIBA does not act as a trade union and does not negotiate the pay and conditions of its salaried members. Consequently it is open to the charge, fairly or otherwise, that it is run for the benefit of the minority of its members who are principals. The sector of the profession most suited to collective bargaining, and thus to trade union membership, is the public sector. The largest trade union is UNISON (formerly NALGO).

Architects' fees

Architects increasingly have to tender for work, sometimes on a percentage basis, sometimes on a lump-sum or time-charged basis, very often for a partial service only – for example scheme design or production information. In place of a mandatory or recommended fee scale, the RIBA now publishes 'Guidance for Clients on Fees'.

Architects' liability for building failures

Until 1977 there was very little public discussion on liability. The bombshell was the case of Ann's and Others *v*. the London Borough of Merton. Traditionally architects have been a little embarrassed at the mention of the topic of liability for building failures because it implies that some architects make mistakes. But no self-respecting architect would want his client to suffer for an error on his part. However, that was all very well in the past when buildings were put together on site under the eye of the architect and by tradesmen who were generally of high skill. Nowadays large sections of a building are often fabricated off-site and erected by unskilled labour. Moreover, the variety of techniques used is so great that the architect would need to be a specialist in a hundred different occupations to be competent to judge the adequacy of everything which goes into a building and for which, in his role of project leader, he is at least partly responsible and for which he is likely to be sued if anything goes wrong.

However, the significance of Ann's *v.* Merton, which did not even involve an architect but a building control officer, was that it changed what everyone had thought was the law, namely that the architect's liability was for six years from when the building is completed, to six years from when the defect becomes manifest. Thus clients might even be able to claim off the estate of a dead architect. Professional indemnity insurance might often be inadequate as it is valid only for the year in which the premium is paid, so that if an architect had ever been in practice on his own account he would have to keep up an insurance for ever. Unfortunately for the architect, it is much more common for people to sue now than it was in the past. However, subsequent case law has taken a much less onerous view of architects' liability in tort. The clients' response has been to bind architects to them with contracts called collateral warranties, and architects' liability for building failures still remains one of their biggest worries.

RIBA code of professional practice

For many years three principles were considered of paramount importance in ensuring the professional status of the architect. These are: that an architect shall be personally responsible for any mistakes he or his employees make and be unable to limit his liability by practising as a limited company; that he shall not advertise; and that he shall compete for work on the basis of quality, not price.

Traditionally this meant that architects could not be directors of limited companies engaged in building contracting or property development; that in addition to not being able to advertise in the local press they could not even have their name plates outside their offices in letters more than 5 centimetres high; and that they had to charge fees in accordance with the mandatory fee scale. This has changed dramatically in recent years, brought about by (i) a ruling by the Monopolies Commission that the mandatory fee scale was not in the public interest, and (ii) a lawsuit (Ann's *v.* Merton) which greatly extended the time limit during which architects are legally liable for any defects in a building for which they are responsible.

The abandonment of these principles, and in particular the abandonment of the mandatory fee scale, has led, in the deep and prolonged recession of the 1990s, to a collapse in fee income and acute financial difficulties for many architects.

The present RIBA code also consists of three principles, which are expanded and interpreted by a number of rules and notes.

Principle one

A member shall faithfully carry out his duties applying his knowledge and experience with efficiency and loyalty towards his client or employer, and being mindful of the interests of those who may be expected to use or enjoy the product of his work.

Principle two

A member shall, at all times, avoid any action or situation which is inconsistent with his professional obligations or which is likely to raise doubts about his integrity.

Principle three

A member shall in every circumstance conduct himself in a manner which respects the legitimate rights and interests of others.

Architects' registration

Since the 1930s architects have had registration of title (see page 17), however, there is no registration of function. There is no particular job – for example, submitting planning applications – which can only be done by an architect. Registration is open to UK residents who have passed (or gained exemption from) the

RIBA exams. ARB also has a code of conduct to which members must adhere and a disciplinary procedure. The purpose of the disciplinary procedure is to protect the public both from ARB members who fall short of their duties and from non-ARB members purporting to be architects. ARB also has joint responsibility with the RIBA for architectural education. Prospective students should check that the school at which they intend to study is recognised both by the RIBA and ARB.

Case Study

Sarah has now completed her architectural studies and is working for a private practice in London.

'At school I liked drawing and making things and wanted to be like my Uncle David, a model engineer who abandoned the family farm in order to pursue his hobby full time.

Outside school time and in the holidays, I tried various labour-intensive jobs. It was not until just after my O-Levels that I found my first real job in the drawing office of a York-based company, SH Construction.

During my three months at this large, innovative and organised design and build company, I assisted the sole female on the technical staff, an artist. The business of procuring jobs/buildings was our focus. We made tender documents and presentation materials, with the best resources available. After some introductory training, I could make measured perspectives, set pages, do some drawing tasks and "publish" a document.

We served a design office containing about 30 architects and numerous other staff. Projects included modern new buildings and interiors around the country including a seemingly endless stream of "sheds". No job was priced at less than £5,000,000, nor had any architect in the office less than ten years' experience.

The output of the company made me aware of various constraints on the design/construction process and has led me to be less unreservedly critical. It was not the design quality that impressed me particularly, but the attitude of the brothers who still run SH Construction. Their straight talking and commitment to innovation impressed me then, and these qualities are frequently mentioned in connection with SH by architects who have worked with them more recently.

Working in such a business-like environment as this taught me what standards were expected when very large sums of money are at stake, and the importance of good marketing. SH was my first experience of architects and their culture: the people I met here convinced me to apply to college to study architecture.

My first year at Cambridge was about exploration and I enjoyed myself very much. To balance this, I assisted on various conservation schemes involving a number of different sorts of exploratory work. Much time was spent in and on various timber-framed mediaeval buildings and churches, with surveying, inspecting work and running errands.

Due to my previous experience, I was able to draw up plans, sections and elevations for reports and planning permission, and also to make 3D drawings. The revelation of mysteries inherent in a seemingly ordinary building fascinated me, but, at Cambridge, there was little opportunity to follow up this interest.

In 1991 I began my year out work at the JRH Partnership in London. The practice's work fell into three categories: large mixed developments for developer clients; work for the Home Office (eg, Strangeways Prison rebuild); and smaller jobs, usually involving listed buildings. All the work in the third category fell to the team I was on, self-sufficient and the smallest in the building, comprising an architect, a technician and myself, working for one of the practice's co-founders.

In the big office in the West End, I was as detached from the construction process as it was possible to be. The compensation was that I was put to work on three schemes, all of which required me to be critical of the apparent restraints governing the project. In addition, the human scale and the needs of the client had to be considered most carefully.

A large part of the year was spent detailing joinery, plaster work, finishes and services for the rebuild of a grade 1 listed house just outside London, and working on designs for the renovation and change of use of flats in Grosvenor Square. Unusually for such a practice, all the team took a part in and discussed freely the administration of the various contracts. The team leader encouraged this discussion: it kept us informed, allowed contributions and reinforced teamwork.

The office culture was a big influence on me, having become my new family. All work had to be done perfectly and fast. Great store was laid on being "good", so I watched out to see what this meant. Most people were working on the North Quay project, worth £3.5 billion. On several occasions I assisted this team, machine-like in its operation, and discovered the stringent demands of such a way of working. In February, the job was shelved and the entire team was made redundant with no warning. For the next six months we expected a redundancy notice every weekend.

The effect of this instability on the output of the practice was radical, but on the surface work appeared to go on as normal. Due to the insecurity and because of the personal demands of commercial work, many employees had a hobby or skill which could be turned into a living if need be.

I developed an alternative career as a graphic designer, training part-time and serving the ultra-low budget sector as I had at school and college. Ruthless programming was needed to make money.

Having chosen not to return to Cambridge for the diploma, I enrolled at the Bartlett School. The first days there introduced me to a pace that has not let up since. I had an idea that my previous experience had only allowed a very partial view and the tutors were keen to confirm this doubt (and to expand my "critical perspective").

Perhaps as a reaction to what I perceived as a tendency towards abstraction in commercial work, I began making work at 1:1 scale in order to communicate my ideas better.

The fifth year, in contrast to the pre-diploma year, was very specific in intent, concerned with three projects to design buildings: a three-bedroom house on a suburban site; a public lavatory in a shopping centre; and a maternity hospital on that same site. While writing my technical dissertation about surgery on buildings, I was supervised both at Arups and Price and Myers Consulting Engineers, undertaking research at the ISE. I learned about the potential role of the engineer in the design process, not something I would see in practice until my case study project.

Unit 18 in 1992–3 was close knit. The end of year show, inside two massive packing crates, was a genuine group effort where the thoughts and efforts of the entire group worked together to achieve a single end. Unit 22 in 1994 was more a unit of individuals. The potential chaos of the diploma show was avoided when a single individual took the lead and the rest of the unit followed. The result, *sans* democracy, was very effective.

Everyone's definition of architecture is inevitably highly personal. The course years were valuable because there was time to discover other ways of doing things, without having to make value judgements. I was to find that many practices are much less open to outside influences, often because they say that they do not have time to investigate. But with each new employer I have gained a new perspective.

When I left college I joined a one-woman practice which had been open for a week. My job was to run small jobs, assist on large jobs, do practice administration (write letters and pay bills) and help establish the office (put up shelves, form a library, design proformas on the computer, etc). The practice specialised in two fields – healthcare and high spec. refurbishments for private clients. Because the practice was small I had a wide variety of experience and because it was new (it is now 12 strong) I saw post-recession business practices in operation.

After a year I was offered a job at GHK Architects. GHK has been in existence for 25 years and I was attracted by their meticulous attitude, the historic buildings work core of their portfolio, the chance to develop their embryonic CAD system and links with their sister company, a worldwide management consultancy. I have now left GHK and joined a high profile practice.'

4 Occupational areas – the jobs

Introduction

The typical architect will spend the first half of his working life as a salaried employee (or hourly-paid freelance) in a large architectural practice and the second half as a self-employed sole principal working from home.

The private sector

The vast majority of architects work either in private sector architectural firms or in public sector authorities. It is impossible to generalise about private sector offices because they range from the 'one-man band' doing mainly small domestic conversions to the big practice designing large commercial developments. In between is a variety of medium-sized practices whose workload may be mainly for private clients or for government authorities. Other private employment covers architects employed by industry, commerce, housing associations, freelance and agency staff. The proportion of architects working in the private sector has been increasing steadily since the late 1970s, and only 17 per cent of architects now work in the public sector.

The public sector

There has been a steady decline in the number of architects working for public sector departments; also, many government agencies such as the Property Services Agency have been privatised. Nevertheless some architects are still employed by, for example, government departments, county councils, local authorities, health authorities and housing associations.

In private practice financial reward is much more varied than in the public sector, the laws of supply and demand at a time of recession tending to keep down the profitability of most practices and the salaries of most employees. However, there are clear compensations in the small office in working in a more informal atmosphere. It is also evident that many architects are prepared to face the hazards of working on their own for very meagre financial rewards. This is probably due in part to the freedom of working for oneself, but also to the expectation of greater rewards in later years if the practice flourishes.

Other activities

Not all architects work in the mainstream of the profession. One in ten work outside it, the most numerous groups being town planning and lecturing. Other activities are writing and journalism, lecturing and landscape architecture. A growing number of architects are involved in a range of consultancy services such as historic buildings or computer services.

Employment

The survey which the RIBA carried out in 1996 showed that there were over 30,000 registered architects, of whom 9 per cent were retired, 4 per cent were unemployed, 9 per cent were working part time and 78 per cent were working full time. However, this masks the full extent of the effect of the recession as 16 per cent of architects in full employment were underemployed. The proportion of sole principals rose rapidly during the recession and there has been a corresponding decrease in the proportion of salaried architects. This is because many architects who have been made redundant have set themselves up as sole principals even though they have found very little work.

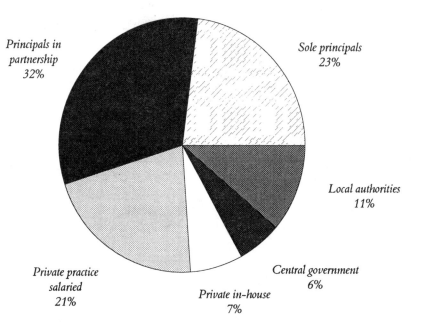

Base: all full-time architects

Figure 4.1   *Architects by field of employment 1996*

Earnings

Architects' earnings are low compared with most other professions. Over the last 15 years they have risen roughly in line with inflation. They increased sharply during the boom years of the late 1980s but have fallen throughout the recession. The average salary in 1996 was £25,000.

Fringe benefits, bonus payments and holidays

The most common benefits offered are a contributory pension, subscriptions to ARB or the RIBA and a company car. At present, less than a quarter of architects receive a bonus; the average bonus value is less than £1,000. The average holiday entitlement is 23 working days, with architects in the public sector receiving more holidays than those in private practice.

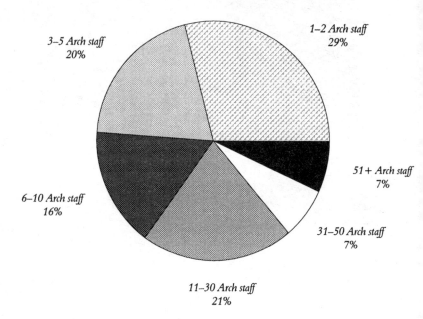

Base: all full-time architects in private practice

Figure 4.2   *Architects by practice size★ 1996*

★ie number of architectural staff

Table 4.1 Structure of the profession

No of architects in calendar year:	Last Two Decades					Last Three Years		
	1970	1975	1980	1985	1990	1994	1995	1996
No. on ARCUK register	21900	25300	27000	29100	31400	30600	30500	30500
% Overseas	6	7	7	8	8	9	9	9
No. Resident in UK	20600	23500	25100	26800	28900	27800	27800	27700
% Retired	7	9	10	10	12	15	13	9
No. in workforce	19100	21400	22600	24100	25400	23600	24100	25200
% Unemployed	1	1	1	1	1	8	3	4
% Not working for other reasons	1	1	1	2	2	2	2	2
% Part-time	2	4	4	5	7	9	10	9
% Women	3	5	6	7	9	9	11	10
No. in full-time employment	18400	20100	21200	22200	22900	19400	20500	21900
% Sole principals	30	31	30	33	39	20	25	23
% Principals in partnership						25	26	32
% Salaried in practice	19	21	22	24	28	25	21	21
% Private in-house	8	5	5	8	8	7	9	7
% Public sector	43	43	43	35	25	24	19	17
% Full-time but underemployed	n/a	n/a	n/a	15	5	19	21	16
No. fully employed	n/a	n/a	n/a	18900	21800	15700	16200	18400

* Estimates based on the register held by the Architects Registration Board of the United Kingdom on 1 January, and the annual RIBA survey of registered architects held on 1 April.

Table 4.2 Median earnings by age and field of employment 1996

Employment field (£)	<30	30-34	35-39	40-44	45-49	50-54	55-59	60-64	65+
Private practice									
Sole principals	n/a	15500	20000	23000	22000	22000	18000	18000	18000
Principals in partnership	n/a	25000	24000	32500	29250	32000	34000	24200	14500
Salaried	16200	20000	23400	26450	25200	27500	25500	n/a	n/a
Private in-house	17000	25000	25000	29000	32500	33950	n/a	32000	n/a
Local authorities	n/a	21000	22500	25000	26100	26200	26200	25450	n/a
Central government	n/a	n/a	24600	27000	32500	33000	29000	n/a	n/a
Total	17000	20000	23450	27000	26900	28500	25400	24000	18000
% Change 1995-96	-1	0	+3	+8	0	+4	+2	-4	+20

Table 4.3   *Median earnings by size of practice*

No of architectural staff (£)	Sole principals	Principals in partnership	Private practice salaried
1–2	19200	18750	20000
3–5	25000	25000	19200
6–10	30000	30000	20000
11–30	n/a	40000	22500
31–50	n/a	50000	25000
51+	n/a	50000	26750
TOTAL	20000	28500	25000

Case Study

Ben, *who works for a high profile practice in London, describes the various stages of training and getting work.*

'My parents had always encouraged me to sketch and paint and at school I did well in most subjects, so when the time came to make a decision on a career, architecture and graphic design were first in my mind. With encouragement from my family and the art teacher at school, I applied to a number of schools including Brighton Polytechnic.

The course at Brighton was well structured with the basics in drawing skills linked to the study of chosen buildings in and around Brighton. We began the year with a project to design a 3 x 3 metre personal space and an architecture centre for a flat, open common in Brighton.

The second year was altogether more successful than the first with more defined projects. Our tutor encouraged us not only to satisfy the basic requirements of the Building Regulations within our schemes but also to be confident of our reasons for the design. I experimented with different forms of architecture with the impression that by the final project in the third year I would be confident and knowledgeable enough to design and communicate exactly what I wanted to.

Before the final year of the degree I worked for my grandfather's Nottingham practice through the summer holiday. Previously, during my A-levels, I had worked in his London office. This was great – at the age of 16 I drew proposed elevations for a mews house in

Chelsea and followed it through to pre-submission planning meetings.

The London office was less commercial but dealt with small but well-funded projects. While in Nottingham I learned a great deal about traditional methods of building and the problems involved with trying to reproduce existing details through surveying existing buildings. The main problem was the cost involved and the lack of experienced craftsmen available to carry out the work. I also worked on large industrial units being developed in the area and was again surprised at how much preparation and production of information was required even for what was essentially a large steel framed building with brick and profiled steel cladding. Here I came to understand the importance of meeting deadlines for tender packages.

When I returned to Brighton my draughting skills had dramatically improved, which gave me confidence to start to experiment with my design. For my final year project we had to choose our own site and brief. I thought that a green-field site with no restrictions would give me the chance to really experiment with building form. This turned out to be a really difficult task. Restrictions of physical boundaries within a site along with a well structured brief could have made life a lot easier at that stage.

I gained a 2:1 honours degree and left Brighton in July 1991 to take part in the European Association of Student Architects annual summer workshop in Kolumna, Russia. This was a thoroughly exciting summer where I met architectural students from all over the world in this small town with a marine base sited on the River Moscow and the River Kolumna. We worked on many projects around the town such as renovating a derelict shop on the main street into a cafe.

I could have stayed in Moscow for a longer period but before I left for Russia I had secured a year out placement with Abba architects in North London. We were already into the recession and, having heard stories of my contemporaries working in pastry factories and selling women's tights, I was happy to join an architect's practice even if I was not too sure of their current situation.

The company was made up of the principal, an architectural assistant, an interior designer and myself. I worked on a number of projects including feasibility reports for new offices for a printer in Ruislip and a new office development in Richmond. I was entrusted with the designs and was encouraged to form a close relationship with the clients and planning consultants. I did feel that I was given a lot of responsibility at this stage. Sadly the office development in Richmond did not go further than the planning stage. The planning consultant and the planners were happy with the scheme but the chairman of the local residents group, who knew a lot of the planning committee, was not. The scheme was rejected and this was not a good time for a small office to lose a large job. I was made redundant with four weeks notice. This was the first time I had experienced rejection in the workplace, and knowing that it had been caused by the action of local politics on the planning committee put me right off the construction industry and architecture.

I wasted no time in finding a job within another vocation, television. I worked for six months at LH Television making coffee. But I learned a lot about how shows are put together and was fascinated by the speed with which a programme is produced from concept to screening. I made a lot of friends during the time in television and spent time in each area deciding which way I would like to work my way up. At that time LH Television was doing a lot of work with LWT and I became friendly with one or two of their set designers. I was offered the opportunity to join their team, only to lose the opportunity when they all lost their jobs a week later.

While still working for LH Television I got together with a friend. He was seriously playing with the idea of setting up a student magazine for architects with the aim of joining together students from schools throughout the country and perhaps the world, so that ideas could be shared and discussed. We both worked in the evenings and late into the night putting together a business plan and developing the main format for the magazine. I was still working for LH Television and becoming more and more disillusioned with the television industry. It was while working on the magazine that I realised the scope and range of subjects that architecture embraced and that the opportunity to explore new ideas to do with society, technology and the future could be expressed and discussed through architecture. It was at this time that I decided to try and work for a practice again.

An old friend of my parents suggested I apply to RMS. As I walked into the RMS offices I realised that this was a place where pride was taken in quality of work and design right down to the office they worked in themselves. The atmosphere was of dedication and underlying excitement for the innovative ideas that were being created and developed. Our meeting went well and I was offered a job with the practice. The activity and the buzz of this office was hugely encouraging and I decided I wanted to work for them. RMS had suffered along with many other practices during the recession and reduced in size from 50 to just 12. The day I started, I was given an immediate project – I had two hours to put together a communal atrium entrance scheme for a residential warehouse conversion in East London. The presentation went well and this became my first job for RMS.

The Associate in charge of the job had a tough task with a very demanding client and hence had little time to spend helping me through the early detail design stages of the project. The main problem I had was relating changes to materials in the design to changes in cost. The atrium was over budget and the client was not prepared to fund the atrium from savings made elsewhere in the scheme, so when the atrium works began on site, I did not follow it through and began working on other projects in the office. These included schemes for a hotel in Jeddah, the early stages of a building for the Institute of Child Health and a large fit out for a firm of solicitors. My involvement in these jobs ranged from presentations, detail packages and tender packages. However, after I had been at RMS for nearly a year I was laid off along with two associates and two other staff.

I had already decided to return to college in September to begin my Part 2 diploma course. I had always wanted to stay in London and so I applied to the Bartlett. I was extremely pleased when I was given a place for the September start. Meanwhile, I had been re-employed at RMS architects. These last seven months at RMS were spent working on two cafes and a number of other jobs including one for CW Accountants.

After passing the pre-diploma I again joined RMS for the summer term and worked on renovating an office for a firm of solicitors. While studying I had also been assisting the principal of NY Design with surveying and draughting and when I left the Bartlett he offered me work.

After two months I realised that I missed being in an office which had several jobs on its books. The opportunity of an interview came up and while I was contemplating this, RMS rang me to offer me a position there. I began by looking after a number of jobs while the project architects took their vacations. I remained on one job, a residential conversion, completing the construction drawings and taking part in design team meetings and site meetings once the job went on site.

Over the last 13 months I have been involved in many other projects, among which are the residential conversion of an old Victorian school in Highgate, and the conversion of a six-storey office building in the City. I am currently working on a detailed design report for upgrading the existing buildings of a university and new recreational areas for staff and students.

I am enjoying working for RMS again and would like to remain here for some time as their clients are usually chosen to be compatible with their philosophies, and therefore work can be produced to maximum effect for both sides. I would eventually like to have my own practice based in London along with certain friends I have met over the years.'

5 Allied professions

Other design disciplines

Landscape architect

Landscape architecture is a design discipline closely related to architecture. In fact one side of the work, the design of hard landscape such as paved areas, is equally the province of both professions. At the other end of the scale it merges with horticulture. Like architects, landscape architects carry out design, detailing and project management. The Landscape Institute was founded in 1929 as the Institute of Landscape Architects. It now has landscape scientists and landscape managers as well as landscape architects. Although one-third of all new students are architects (the next largest group is geographers), architects do not gain any special exemption from the Landscape Institute exams. Students take the exams of a college with a recognised course. This can be as a first degree or postgraduate course following a relevant degree. Undergraduate courses are three or four years, some with a year in a work placement. Postgraduate study is two years full-time or three or four years part-time. You must then do two years' professional practice before taking the professional practice exam.

Landscape architecture is a small profession with only 200 people qualifying each year. The exams consist of written papers and testimonies of study (ie design projects). A typical syllabus is history of landscape and gardens, theory of landscape design, plant soils and cultivation, construction, ecology, plants and planting, advanced theory and practice of landscape design, the law relating to landscape.

The Landscape Institute

The recognised professional qualification for landscape architects, scientists and managers is Associate of the Landscape Institute (ALI), a qualification of equivalent status to professionally qualified architects, civil engineers and quantity surveyors. The means of obtaining that qualification vary for the different divisions because specific higher education courses in landscape sciences do not exist at present. However, all applicants must first attain graduate membership of the Institute, complete the necessary professional experience, and pass the Institute's professional practice examination before being elected to Associate membership of any division. The regulations and syllabus for this examination are fully set out in the *Examinations Handbook* which is supplied free to members on joining the Institute but which may also be purchased from RIBA Publications Ltd, Finsbury Mission, Moreland Street, London EC1V 8VB.

Job opportunities

There is a steady demand for landscape professionals, both at home and overseas, many of whom work as private consultants receiving commissions from public authorities or private clients; others are directly employed by government departments, public bodies, local authorities, industry and new town development corporations.

Salaries are comparable with those of other professions, such as architects, civil engineers and town planners, as can be seen from the advertisements for appointments in the Institute's journal *Landscape Design* and associated supplements.

Information

Contact the Landscape Institute if you require membership application papers (indicating the division(s) you are interested in), or if you require answers to specific questions.

Interior designer

Interior design is also a design discipline. The main difference between what the interior designer does and what the architect does is that the former works within the building itself and is thus even more concerned than the architect with detail design. The work of the interior designer is almost entirely confined to the private sector and is concerned largely with interiors of public buildings and the design of exhibitions. The training of the interior designer is part of the art and design educational system. This is described in the companion volume *Careers in Art and Design*. There is a wide variety of different branches of design and so you might also like to consider other fields such as furniture or product design.

Postgraduate courses are available, for example, at the Royal College of Art. The professional body for designers is the Chartered Society of Designers (CSD) founded in 1930. As interior designer is not a restricted title, members of the Institute call themselves Chartered Designers. Interior design is an attractive area of further study for architects because it is not necessary to attend any further college courses. Entry to the various classes of corporate membership of CSD is by portfolio and *viva voce*. Requirements for membership are set out in *Careers in Art and Design*. CSD has never placed restrictions on its members practising as limited companies.

Other building professions

Surveyor

Whereas the root of architecture is design, the root of surveying is measurement. There are many types of surveying – not all of them concerned with buildings. However, the branches of surveying most closely allied to architecture are building and quantity surveying. Much of the work of the building surveyor is concerned with routine maintenance, but in the refurbishment of buildings the building surveyor performs a job virtually identical to that of the architect, and sometimes works alongside him in multidisciplinary teams.

On the other hand the quantity surveyor performs a specialist role, that of producing bills of quantities, and his is a profession peculiar to the British way of building. The purpose of bills of quantities is to produce a document which all builders tendering for a particular job can price against, thus avoiding the duplication involved in each builder measuring off the architect's drawings. This is something of a mixed blessing, however, as often the detailed specification is drawn up by the quantity surveyor when it is really the architect's job. The traditional method of working is for tenderers to price bills of quantities and working drawings. However, in commercial work, various 'fast track' methods are now used to save time, many of which originated in North America. These include producing priced specifications instead of bills of quantities and doing most of the working drawings after the job is priced. As well as producing bills of quantities the QS also provides general advice on cost matters; this is an aspect of his work which has grown in recent years. With design and build the quantity surveyor is often the employer's agent and produces a specification document called the employer's requirements. The professional body for surveyors is the Royal Institution of Chartered Surveyors.

Engineer

Engineering is a science-based discipline concerned with theoretical and mathematical calculation. There are many different kinds of engineer, only a very few of whom are concerned with buildings. There is no general engineer as there is architect or surveyor.

The structural engineer's training is concerned largely with man-made materials such as steel or reinforced concrete which are specifically made to have the properties of strength that the engineer assumes in his calculations. The aim of structural design is economy. However, with traditional materials, engineer-designed structures are frequently over-designed, compared with rule-of-thumb designs on the basis of an architect's or builder's experience, because the engineer is obliged to design to codes of practice and to take a pessimistic evaluation of the strength of materials such as timber which varies greatly from one piece to another. Structural engineers are less often used on work to existing buildings most of which, although they are in no danger of collapsing, do not conform to present-day codes. On the other hand, with other projects such as industrial plants the project is largely engineering-based with very little input from the architect. The professional institute for structural engineers is the Institute of Structural Engineers.

Electrical and mechanical engineers are responsible for the design of services within buildings, such as lighting and heating. The professional institute for electrical and mechanical engineers is the Chartered Institute of Building Services Engineers.

Town planner

The town planning profession originally developed out of the architectural profession and, to a lesser extent, surveying and engineering. There are more architect/town planners than any other dual qualification involving an architect. However, this applies mainly to the older members of the profession, and nowadays only a small proportion of the intake of planning students are architects, whereas over 50 per cent do either an undergraduate planning course or an undergraduate course in one of the social sciences (geography, economics or sociology) followed by a planning course. The biggest group is geographers.

In the 1950s the Royal Town Planning Institute made a conscious decision to stop being a design-based discipline and become oriented towards the social services, but planners have retained their statutory powers to comment on architects' schemes submitted for planning permission – although the final decision is, of course, taken by the elected members.

An architect has no more exemption from planning courses than is given to any other graduate. After passing RIBA Part 3 he must do either a two-year full-time or a three-year part-time course followed by two years' practical experience in town planning. Additionally, there are several 'dual routes' available leading to qualifications in both planning and architecture.

There are over 500 government, local authority and development corporation offices in which planners are employed. The majority of planners in Britain are employed by these public authorities. However, in recent years there has been a considerable growth in the number of planners working as planning consultants and in other agencies. These range from one person to large firms with international offices and now there are over 1100 firms.

Architectural technologist

Architectural technologists, also called architectural technicians, specialise in the technological aspects of building. They work with architects and other professionals on building projects, either in architectural practices or, for example, local authority planning departments. They may also set up in practice either on their own or with other professionals.

The professional body for architectural technologists is the British Institute of Architectural Technologists. The forerunner of this, the Society of Architectural and Associated Technicians, was set up in 1965 as an associate society to the RIBA.

The term architectural technician is often used to describe anyone in an architectural practice or department who is not a qualified architect or other professional. They generally, but by no means always, work at an intermediate or junior level and are less likely to work as designers than qualified architects are. However, membership of the British Institute of Architectural Technologists is a professional qualification in its own right which is open to those who satisfy the educational requirements for entry to an approved course.

How to become a member

Standard route
You must have gained one of the following qualifications:

◆ a degree in architectural technology or a built environment subject with a technology base.

- ◆ an approved BTEC HNC/HND in building studies.
- ◆ an alternative BIAT approved higher level qualification. (A directory of approved courses is available from BIAT.)

In addition, you need to complete a two-year practice qualification logbook under the supervision of an approved supervisor. A further year of work experience will be required for those who have followed a full-time course of study. You must also pass a professional interview.

There are a number of non-standard routes to becoming a member, details of which can be obtained from BIAT. In addition to Members, BIAT has Associates, Students and Retired Members.

Postgraduate training

Postgraduate courses are available at most architectural schools. Subjects available include the following: urban and regional planning, urban design, urban revitalisation, landscape design, architectural conservation, building science, building services engineering, interior design, housing, energy and environmental impact studies, history and theory of architecture, building economics, management, computer-aided design, health facility planning, environmental psychology, construction management, planning for leisure.

Full-time courses are usually for one or two years; part-time courses are usually longer. You will have to find out from the particular school whether you can get a grant.

Continuing professional development

The RIBA requires all members to undertake a minimum of 35 hours of continuing professional development (CPD) study a year and to keep a record that they are doing so. They will be expected to draw up a personal development plan in consultation with a fellow member. The RIBA has not opted for a highly structured CPD curriculum; it has produced a broad framework for suggested CPD studies, but at the core of the scheme is each member's obligation to pursue his personal professional development. A mix of activities is recommended including participation in study groups, using open learning packages, job-related research, personal research, teaching, journalism and relevant committee work.

6 Getting started

Should you work in an architect's office before starting college?

A student must have two years' practical experience before talking Part 3. One year must be after taking Part 2; the other year may be taken any time after a student has started his course and is generally referred to as 'the year out'. Practical experience taken before starting a course does not count.

If, however, you are unsure of whether you want to be an architect, a short period in an architect's office may help you to make up your mind. Other than that, working in an architect's office at this stage has no particular benefit over any other activity which you might do between secondary school and college, such as working on a building site or travelling abroad. However, a gap of, say, a year between school and architectural college would benefit most people.

During periods of practical experience, a student is normally required to maintain a log book, or RIBA Practical Training Record Sheet to give its full name. This must be signed monthly by the student's supervising architect, and every three months by his practical training adviser.

The year out

The year out during the course may be strictly supervised by the college both with regard to when it is taken and which employer to work for, or it may be left to the individual student. At this stage the student will probably be flung from grand student ideas of replanning the universe to office junior sharpening the pencils. Almost all experience at this stage is, in retrospect, valuable. However, few employers are prepared to offer an inexperienced student, coming for the very brief (from the employer's point of view) period of a year, the sort of experience that he will find rewarding.

However, the goal is now to pass Part 3 and this requires actual experience in job running. This means that experience must be gained working on a building which is on site, increasingly taking over the duties of the job architect. The smaller private office with a rapid turnover of varied projects has much to offer at this stage in a student's training.

Case Study

Steve *has now completed his diploma and works for a 'big name' London practice, but he found getting work in his year out more difficult than he had expected.*

'My search for work started with small offices. I decided that I didn't want to work for any of the named practices, the main reason being that the experience of my final degree year left me feeling I was not good enough. However, I took a very arrogant attitude to the small offices, spurred on by stories of how the previous year's students had had to think hard about which job offer to choose. I sent out a few grotty CVs and standard letters and had two interviews and one job offer. This job would have involved a lot of travelling and paid just over half as much as I was used to. After writing to ask if they would put the amount up the job offer was withdrawn.

Up to this time I had allowed myself the comfort of thinking, though not completely consciously, that my life would progress along the course I had now set it on: three years at college, one year out earning money in practice, two years back at college, work, Part 3, work, my own office. It was now becoming clear that life was not that reliable.

In the final term of my degree the recession really hit. Suddenly all my phone calls received negative responses and my pile of rejection letters grew. My search expanded and I resorted to just going alphabetically through the RIBA index.

College finished, the summer passed, and I still had no job. Some people who I had graduated with still had their jobs. Others had been made redundant. At Christmas I gave up looking for architectural employment.

During the time I was not completely idle. In October I had been asked by a friend in the same position to help hang a students' exhibition at the 9H gallery with a few others from our year. This mainly involved a lot of decorating but I did get to decide on how some of the areas I was working on were hung.

Come the next exhibition the others who I had originally been asked to help out were not available, so I was therefore able to have a lot more involvement in how the exhibition came together. The rest of my world at this time had little to do with architecture, so it was good to feel useful in the subject in which I was trained. Sadly this was the last exhibition the 9H was putting on for six months, so I had to find alternative employment.

As promised, by the end of June the 9H gallery was back again and had now become The Architecture Foundation. I called and offered my services and in the time before going back to do my diploma I was able to work on two exhibtions and look after the gallery during the weekends.

With the money I had earned here and a donation from my mother I was able to Interail around Europe, rejuvenating my interest in architecture. I had already done this tour after my first year, though my knowledge and desire to learn then were still not fully developed. This time I was determined to visit all those buildings that had been just around the corner and spend the money to actually go in to the museums. I travelled alone for the first three weeks with a modern architecture in Europe guide book and my camera.

After college the recession was still biting deep so I signed on at the unemployment office as there was still not much point in even thinking of trying for proper architectural employment. This was my busiest period, however. Although I started every week thinking I only had my two regular days with the gallery, the phone would always ring and I would end up working six or seven days a week.

The exhibition coordinator at the gallery at this time was the daughter of a well-known architect. I was asked to assist her mother in the design and management of renovations to her house. It was while still working on this project that her mother asked me if I would come into the office to help out for a couple of weeks on some work for the Glyndebourne Opera House. Two and a half years later I am still there.'

7

Top tips for getting into architecture

for Getting into Architecture

◆ Work experience at school. Find out what goes on in an architect's office before committing yourself any further. During your last year at school you should be offered two weeks' work experience arranged through the school.

◆ Work in an architect's office when a student. Before qualifying you must work for two years in an architect's office. Short periods do not count but by working in the holidays you will gain office skills and supplement your grant.

◆ Do your final year thesis on a subject of interest to the office you want to join.

◆ Produce a professional-looking curriculum vitae. Bear in mind that architects' CVs are a bit different. The best ones interleave drawings with text. Your college Part 3 tutor may be able to help you with examples.

◆ Build up the skills useful to an office employing students. Are you CAD literate? Can you do presentation drawings?

◆ Obtain practical knowledge of construction. Get a holiday job working on a building site.

◆ Cultivate your own clients. Beware of doing private jobs before you have the necessary experience, but this is a good way of learning and building up a client base. If the job is too large to do in your spare time, bring it into the practice.

Case Study

Christopher *found the answer to getting a job after his diploma year was to form a practice with his father.*

'The recession struck immediately I left college in 1992, with full-time employment being virtually impossible to obtain. Later in the year my father took voluntary redundancy and we decided to set up our own practice, The Wilson Partnership. It seemed a good combination: we were at different stages in our careers, with 38 years' experience in architecture from my father, and fresh ideas, enthusiasm and energy from myself. I also had a certain amount of experience in small business from working at Cedric Price Architects.

A practice that begins in the middle of a recession has a good foundation to start from, as things will only be able to improve, and you develop a resilient attitude. We had already reduced our cost of living, which meant we did not require a vast amount of work. This was fortuitous as the slow workload meant we were able to develop our library of materials, equipment, our experience at working on small projects, and to build up speed gradually.

Our knowledge of running a business was heightened by attending a course where we learnt the various business aspects, from marketing to tax, including cash-flow forecasts, profit and loss tables, and produced our own business plan. The course helped us to understand the pragmatic side of a business, but also enabled contact with other new local businesses. Most importantly, it helped in knowing that other people were at the same stage as ourselves.

During the first year we concentrated on small projects requiring planning permission and Building Regulation approvals. Thus we were constantly updating our knowledge on the current regulations and Unitary Development Plans of local authorities. Most of the work was single-storey extensions.

In our second year we aimed at becoming more efficient in our work. We decided to test the volume of work we could sensibly cope with, which in turn would supply a better service to our clients. We found that, to a certain extent, we worked more efficiently with a larger workload, and that it was best to utilise the eight weeks the planners took, and the five weeks the building control took, to stagger the projects. Dealing with a number of projects at the same time was unnerving at first. However, once we became used to the procedures it added variety to the work, and ideas on one project began to inform others. We were acquiring larger, two-storey extension projects, which were technically more challenging, and in planning terms more complicated. We had previously worked out our own structural calculations, but were now using a structural engineer for the complicated structural problems.

The scale and quality of projects grew in the third year. This was possibly due to people becoming used to the economic situation, and definitely due to our increased confidence in obtaining projects. We were learning how to communicate with the local authority, and completing the work to our and the clients' satisfaction within a reasonable period of time. If the building process is too painfully long for a client, they will not build again or recommend us to their friends or associates, so we try to work within the agreed project period. Now the company is going from strength to strength, with a number of JCT minor works contracts, and we are looking for larger commissions as well as more small ones. Most of our work is in Harrow, expanding into Brent and Ealing. Our main aim is to work more in central and south London using my flat in south London as a second office. We are planning to build a conservatory at the back of the Harrow office with an extension at the side to provide space for our expanding library and computer areas and a pleasant area for meetings.'

Case Study

Mark completed his diploma studies and set about looking for a job. Finding work scarce at home, he decided to try working abroad.

'I had been put in touch with BGKK, a practice based in Berlin, through a contact in England. Three of the partners had worked for Fosters in England and the other in Rogers' office. They were all under 30 and had come back to Germany after having won a competition for a headquarters building for a private gas company a few miles from the city of Leipzig. They had interviewed me upon my arrival in Berlin but had no vacancies at that time. This time I was lucky.

There are a great number of architects in Germany who rely upon competitions not only for work but to survive. Architects are normally paid to enter competitions organised by the chamber or local organisation of architects. In most cases, projects over a certain size or of a certain building type are required by law to be offered up for competition – this can either be privately organised or by the chamber itself. This is a very important stepping-stone for young practices to make a name for themselves. I started at BGKK running competitions for them. At this stage they were very small: myself, a student and the four partners.

The first competition was for a hotel in Kopenick, south-east Berlin. The office decided that a number of students would be employed to help with the final presentation drawings. I would work with one of the partners to attain an initial design and then present this to the other three partners. This proved to be a constructive way of working. There was a great deal of cooperation between the partners and it was felt that no allowance should be made for the conservative bodies that controlled planning legislation in Berlin.

In this sense we achieved our intended result. We came last among the five invited architects but were praised in a number of student magazines for our aggressive approach. I had begun to get to know a number of Technical University students, some of whom had helped on competitions. They were very enthusiastic and we felt that the only way to change the planning system was to keep pushing with radical designs. We tried this with another couple of competitions but no promising results were forthcoming.

By this time the office had managed to secure the gas headquarters building and was now expanding to accomplish the detailed design phase of the project. I became involved as I felt that I needed to refresh my detailing skills. Each member of the team was allocated certain packages. I was responsible for the coordination of the 15 different sorts of facades. At the end of this intense period a large book of details was produced that was given to the main contractor to show how the building should be put together. The contractor can differ from these if he feels that the specification can be maintained, and the architect merely retains an "artistic" overview of the proceedings. A large number of German offices work in this manner as it apparently maintains a more profitable profile in terms of fee income and expenditure.

At the end of this period it was felt that the office should try another competition. This was for a 100m span bridge to the west of Berlin. I was eager to take part in the team and was given the project. We formed a liaison with Anthony Hunt Association, Paris branch, as our consultant engineers. After a number of visits to Paris to finalise the design we handed in our 1.5m-long model, along with our drawings, and hoped for the best. Again we were disappointed.

However, the practice was starting to be mentioned much more and we were offered an exhibition of work at the Aedes Gallery in Berlin. At this time the practice had been approached by a local authority which was interested in carrying out a planning exercise for a new civic centre. BGKK presented a town plan for a new town hall, a shopping centre and a private housing development. After the presentation it emerged that the housing developer and the local authority were eager to press ahead with the new town development. After a series of meetings with the developer it was decided that I would act as team leader with one other architect assisting. We proceeded to planning permission and then assessed the situation regarding the housing market.

Planning permission was easily achieved due to an existing housing crisis and the developers were happy with the scheme, so it was decided to press ahead to scheme design. Once this had been achieved it was decided to push through to *Leitdetails* only, the equivalent of design and build. Our role, as the project went ahead for construction, was relatively small. I was, however, able to follow the project through its early phases.

At this point I felt that my Berlin experience had naturally come to an end. My knowledge of the language had improved greatly and I had increased my architectural experience and knowledge. I felt that unless I were to put down permanent roots in Berlin, I would not achieve anything more, and I still felt that I wanted to get back into the scene in London. Having recently married, my wife and I decided to head home.

London felt strange. I had lived and worked in Berlin for two and a half years. I was not sure what the work situation was so I decided to send out my curriculum vitae and hope for the best. Within ten days I had accepted a position at KPF. The mother firm is KPF New York. It had set up an office in England just as the KPF buildings in Canary Wharf had reached completion, and used these as an excellent opportunity to spring into Europe. They had almost immediately won a competition for a site in Berlin as well as a large tower in Frankfurt. Working at KPF has opened up a range of opportunities and contacts that are truly global.'

8 The future of architecture

The British system of architectural practice is based on the arts and crafts tradition, with the architect responsible for the design and construction process. This was encapsulated in the RIBA study, *The Architect and His Office*, written in the early 1960s, which set out the services which an architect provides and how he is remunerated. The recession of the 1990s prompted a new study by the RIBA, called *Strategic Study of the Profession*. This study identified changes in the market, in the commercial environment and in the profession. Clients have become more professional in the way they procure both buildings and design services. They value design, but are increasingly unwilling to accept at face value the forms and terms of service that architects have been accustomed to offer. While popular opinion in an increasingly wealthy and visually aware society is more in tune with design and therefore appreciative of what architects can offer, competition from other professionals is increasing in practically every aspect of architectural services, particularly in the valued role of the strategic adviser to the client and for all aspects of management and control of the production process.

At the same time, big changes have taken place in architectural education. The traditional method of teaching whereby students started designing small buildings and progressed to more complex ones, and in the final year produced a thesis has, particularly in the London schools, been superseded by a unit system of students from more than one year choosing a tutor for the year because of his design philosophy. This has placed a greater emphasis in the schools on design but weakened the technical teaching. A general increase in design skills is greatly to be welcomed, and indeed is strongly reflected in what the public wants from architects, what students want – and architectural education is nowadays driven by student demand rather than the numbers required by the profession – and what the tutors want.

Many of the larger offices now have different teams for conceptual design and production design. Students who leave college with highly developed design skills stand a better chance of getting jobs as conceptual designers. However, as with all arts subjects, the number of such jobs is small and most are poorly paid. If the proportion of construction work undertaken by architects is to be maintained or increased, it is also important that some – possibly a majority – of architectural students concentrate on acquiring practical skills in construction and project management.

However, architectural education does not end with a diploma in architecture. The professional practice exam has become increasingly stiff over the years. In addition, all RIBA members are now required to carry out continuing professional development. The replacement of ARCUK by ARB has led to the formation of a joint RIBA/ARB validation board. Thus while students and colleges are setting increasingly high standards for design, the professional institutions are setting increasingly high standards for practice. Although the RIBA has only one class of corporate membership, it is setting increasingly stiff requirements for RIBA registered practices which, for example, include compulsory professional indemnity insurance. The effect of this, particularly when combined with the uncertain jobs market, is to prolong the time between getting a diploma and taking Part 3.

The 1990s have seen the worst recession since the second world war. Many architects have been made redundant and suffered either unemployment or underemployment. Most architects have suffered a loss in earnings, lack of career progression and a loss of job satisfaction. This is the result of the simultaneous decline of the public and private sectors in architecture together with alternative forms of building procurement such as design and build leading to architects losing their role as automatic leaders of the building team and the workload that went with this. The decline of the public sector has been particularly dramatic and now employs less than half of what it did 20 years ago.

Information technology has revolutionised the way we work. Most drawing is now done on computer rather than on the drawing board. Small offices no longer employ secretaries or receptionists: a word-processor and an answerphone suffice.

Government has forced architects to abandon a mandatory fee scale; the Latham Report, not yet implemented, looks forward to a less adversarial construction industry.

Increasingly architects and architectural students will have to make a choice and to plan their career. Nearly 10 per cent of architects work abroad, an increasing proportion of these in Europe. There is greater specialism. Architects work as developers, facilities managers, consultants, community architects, builders, product designers and in many other fields. The pattern of change is towards portfolio careers. Students will study architecture to Part 1 or Part 2 as a prelude to a career in a different field of design, or a related profession such as landscape architecture.

Architects have been particularly badly affected by the recent recession. Both workload and the public perception of architects are now improving. If this improvement is sustained and if the colleges, the professional bodies and the architectural practices maintain the improvements, the future for architects and architecture could be exciting. If not, we could see a continuation of the 1990s with many architects frustrated by lack of opportunity and poor pay.

Case Study

Jake, who works freelance for a small practice in North London, describes his experiences of diploma school and finding a job.

'I completed my diploma at the University of North London (UNL) in June 1995, having taken my degree at the University of Sheffield. One of the main differences between the structure of design teaching in London and elsewhere in the country is the use by London schools of a unit-based system. Dividing the year into a number of working groups (of around ten students) enables the school to investigate a range of architectural issues in a more coherent and intensive manner than is perhaps possible if all students follow an identical programme or set their own briefs. The unit system was devised by the Architectural Association in the 1970s, and its general adoption has assisted a more open communication between the London schools. The system depends upon the number of young practitioners eager to teach in London, attracted to the capital by its (unquestionably unfair) cultural and economic dominance. Unit-based teaching holds the danger of the individual student feeling restricted, as each unit necessarily works closely to the agenda set by the tutor. Consequently, the single most important decision of the year for the student is the first – which unit to apply to.

When I was at UNL the five units offered a good range of approaches, generally united by a concern with developing socially cohesive environments. The interest of this unit was in developing a topographical approach to design, whereby architectural proposals are closely derived from the existing conditions, both physical and social, of a specific site. In my fourth year, the unit worked on proposals for regenerating an area of Whitechapel, East London, centred around an imposing, derelict Victorian board school. The work of the fifth year adapted from these ideas to a site in the French Alps, aiming at questioning established notions of distinctions between "artificial" and "natural" qualities.

Before starting at UNL, I had spent 18 months working in architectural practices in Berlin, and I returned for the summer after the fourth year. Although this was a very beneficial and enjoyable experience, I decided to work in London for a while after graduating. All of my work in this time had been on a freelance basis for specific short-term projects. Despite the partial recovery of the building market, it is still far from easy to find permanent contractual employment in London. Short-term work does at least give a useful introduction to differing work environments, while making it difficult to accumulate a more substantial experience of practical issues. For freelance work, CAD experience is often invaluable. Producing working drawings for an office is a very different discipline to sketching models in college, but I have been fortunate enough to find practices prepared to let me learn as work proceeds. I have also enjoyed being involved with the building process on site in my current job.

As the "social art", architecture has had quite a hard time in this country since the end of the 1970s, due to the apparent abdication of responsibility by our political leaders to the global market and a seemingly general disinterest in the quality of the built environment. Yet there are signs that the situation is finally starting to improve, with a far more environmentally concerned government, and with such issues the subject of much debate and popular protest. The opportunity to improve our environment in a direct and lasting way is one of the greatest drives to study and work as an architect.'

9 Qualifications available

Introduction

Until the latter part of the nineteenth century the only method of qualification was articled pupillage – a system which is still used by solicitors and chartered accountants. However, many architectural students were not happy with this and in 1847 the Architectural Association was founded to supplement the training provided by articles with evening lectures.

In 1863 the Institute of British Architects set its first exam against the background of widespread opposition of some members, who considered that as architecture is an art an exam was not a suitable test of merit. This exam was purely voluntary and was in technical matters only. The first obligatory exam was in 1882; in the year it gained its Royal Charter, the RIBA introduced a three-stage system of preliminary, intermediate and final exams. The Architectural Association and Liverpool School of Architecture gained exemption from the RIBA intermediate exam in 1902, that is to say the schools' own exams were accepted by the RIBA in lieu of students having to take the RIBA's exam. In 1920 the Architectural Association started the first full-time five-year course. The RIBA also authorised the setting up of sandwich courses with periods in college interspersed with periods in architects' offices.

Full-time courses

In recent years the RIBA has rationalised the different methods of training available. Entry to the RIBA examination in architecture is now normally open to you only if you are attending regular courses in schools of architecture approved by the RIBA: this means courses in schools listed by the RIBA and unrecognised courses in schools which also run recognised courses. You must normally have two A-levels and three GCSEs (or their equivalents), and must have attended a school for at least three years before gaining exemption from RIBA Part 1 and a further two years before gaining exemption from RIBA Part 2. These requirements are for full-time students, who comprise 94 per cent of new entrants to the first year.

Part-time courses

Requirements for part-time students, who comprise 5 per cent of new entrants to the first year, are as for full-time students, except that they must usually attend for four years before gaining exemption from RIBA Part I and a further three years before gaining exemption from RIBA Part 2, and must be employed on a day-release basis.

External exams

The RIBA recognises that some students cannot meet the education and attendance requirements and has established for them a system of special entry to the examination. These students are mature candidates with a high level of practical experience, candidates with other professional or academic qualifications in fields related to architecture, candidates who have attended a recognised school but have had to leave without having passed the school's exams, and candidates who have studied architecture outside the UK but who have been unable to complete a course of study leading to a qualification. These special entry students comprise 1 per cent of new entrants to the first year.

The RIBA has recently revised the pattern of external examinations. The Examination in Architecture establishes a route by which external candidates may seek to qualify as architects. This additional route is based specifically on practice with fewer written papers and project-based assessment. Details of the entry requirements are given in Chapter 10.

Entry requirements for schools of architecture

The list of recognised schools and full details of the minimum entry requirements are set out in Chapter 10. Under certain circumstances it is possible for students of architecture with a high standard of pass in the BTEC National Certificate/Diploma in Building Studies (Architectural) and with the required GCSEs to be considered for an architectural course by the RIBA. Full details of this scheme are also provided in Chapter 10. However, some schools, particularly those which are part of a university, have specific requirements in addition to those of the RIBA. You can obtain these by writing to the school direct. The most common additional requirement is A-level maths.

Although the RIBA allows you to gain exemption from Part 2 after four years' full-time study at a recognised school, most courses are of five years' duration with an additional year of practical experience, generally (although by no means always) after passing Part 1. A further period of at least a year is required, making two years' practical experience in all before you can take the professional practice exam.

Registration by ARB and RIBA membership

When you have passed RIBA Part 3 you are eligible for registration by the Architects Registration Board, provided the school where you gained exemption from RIBA Parts 1 and 2 is recognised by both RIBA and ARB. If you are a member of RIBA, you become a full member and can use the letters RIBA. There is only one class of corporate membership, but those who have enrolled for a recognised course can be student members.

Qualifications

In addition, schools give their own qualifications: either a diploma or a degree, or sometimes both. For example, some university schools award a degree after three years when you have passed Part 1, and a diploma after the final year when you have passed Part 2. However, there is no standard terminology and there is no pecking order of merit between bachelor of arts, bachelor of science or diploma.

Case Study

__Liz__ entered architecture 'by accident' but now really enjoys it, and after passing Part 3 has been made a director of the firm with which she started her year out.

'My arrival in architecture school happened by a lucky chance. Although talented at art in school, I had always aspired to be a lawyer and therefore not taken art at A-Level. However, my science and English grades were not good enough for law, so I applied for architecture at Queen's University in Belfast.

My idea at the beginning of the course was not to continue through to become a qualified architect but simply to do the degree and then go into industry or even transfer to law school. I had no preconceived ideas or expectations. I knew no architects personally or indeed very little about the profession at all. I did, however, know quite a lot about buildings and had travelled to many places abroad, visiting hundreds of towns and buildings.

I entered the start of what was to become my career at the height of the property and development boom, surrounded by optimism, knowing little of what was really involved in achieving architect status.

I began at Queen's in 1988 and left in 1991 and was present during an interesting transition in the development of the department and the country itself. We were tutored by local architects, the "Dublin 5", and at all times were involved in the school's push for wider recognition and competitiveness. All the tutors pushed hard to improve the profile of the department and this led to an exciting and challenging environment.

I became very involved in the social, political and educational spheres and represented my year twice on university and "ArcSoc" committees. During my final year I was secretary to the Architectural Society which was extremely well organised and held a lecture programme even the RIBA would envy!

During the summer of 1989, through a contact with one of the tutors at Queen's, I was given a job offer for summer experience with Consarc Design (CD) in London. This architectural and surveying group had a large office in Belfast and two smaller offices in London. It is interesting to note that in Belfast, CD was considered one of the top five architectural companies, and employed approximately 40 staff, while the offices in London, one primarily building surveyors and the other architects, held a relatively low-profile position.

I was employed alongside a colleague from Queen's who was to do her year out with the firm, and for that summer I experienced the high life of the "boom". I worked under one of the directors and, while spending most of the time in the office, enjoyed observing the operation of the office and project management by taking a keen interest in the day-to-day activities.

By 1991 and graduation, the architectural climate was much changed. All of the 22 in my year who qualified stayed in Ireland or went abroad and only 12 eventually found work. I applied to several practices in London but only received replies from a handful. CD offered me a placement, however, and I quickly accepted.

The year was one of great experience for me, in terms of both the practice and the projects. The company had been forced to merge the two offices into its central London office and had down-sized to eight full-time employees by the time I completed my year. Project-wise, this situation worked in my favour, as many of the smaller jobs in the office came to me. I proceeded to take on quite a lot of responsibility for two smaller jobs on site and was actively involved in specification writing, numerous client presentations, site meetings, job certification and general project management, as well as drawing production.

I decided not to return to Belfast to continue on the Part 2 course. Although my time in Belfast had been so enjoyable, I wanted ultimately to practise in London or Europe and hoped the contacts and experience gained in an English school would be more advantageous.

I applied to ten diploma schools in the UK and accepted an offer from Bath University, which appealed to me because both years were devoted to design projects, Bath had a reputation as one of the top five schools, and I felt confident that I could fit in with the technical experience of the school. I was also allowed to miss the first term (while the other students were on placement) and decided to use the time to travel the world for six months. This was undoubtedly the architectural tour of my lifetime.

The structure of the course at Bath was substantially different to that at Queen's. The two final years were almost entirely design based. Three formal lectures were given each week but no exams taken; a written submission was all that was required.

My thesis was the design of a large wholesale distribution and retail market, based around the concept of water distribution and transport, additional market units, promenades and the reinterpretation of large-scale supermarket principles.

CD asked me to rejoin the practice when I had completed my diploma. CD's London office had shrunk to four but had now expanded to 17, including seven architects, one quantity surveyor and one building surveyor. Each of the three directors focused on creating new client bases. The result is an office with three separate and distinct project "houses" ranging from public sector housing through retail and private clients to extensive refurbishment and commercial jobs.

At CD I have been given growing responsibility for the social and professional well-being of the office. I have organised CPD and social events. We have regular in-house speakers from manufacturing and advisory bodies. Each member of staff now has a "personal" performance and planning evaluation. The process involves an interview with two directors, a detailed analysis, a 12-month plan and a six-month review of the plan.

I have worked on a large number of schemes as well as taking on an increased role in the management of the office and I am now a director of the practice.'

10 Where to study

Introduction

For most students there will be no substitute for a full-time course. However, for those who cannot or do not want to train in this way, a part-time course is clearly the answer. The special entry route to qualification is open to only very few and is really a safety net for those who would otherwise fall through the system.

Some schools will be excluded from your choice, because they have special academic requirements. In some professions, such as medicine, it is the norm for the medical schools to specify exactly what A-levels they require. In architecture there are very few schools which demand more than one specific A-level, and unless these are the A-levels which you have or are intending to study, or unless there is some other overpowering factor for choosing that particular school, you should look elsewhere. These A-levels are demanded as being necessary for the particular course which that school runs, not because they are essential knowledge for becoming an architect.

Grants

Architecture students can expect to receive a five-year mandatory grant towards their studies if they have not received local education authority funding for a previous course. Students should ensure that they do not mistakenly apply for a three-year discretionary award in the first instance.

Do you want to live at home?

You should consider the location of the school at which you want to study – how far it is from your home. You may want to be as far away or as near as possible. Consider also the size of the town or city, too small a town may not provide the range of academic stimulation or social activities. A very large city such as London will provide an enormous range of activities but the school or university will not be the centre of your social life. You will have to make your own circle of friends and you will be less likely to find accommodation in a hall of residence. It is not always true that accommodation is most difficult to find in a large city – although expensive, a private rented sector of housing does exist, whereas some of the newer universities have been set up in towns and cities where this sort of accommodation is in even shorter supply.

University?

Almost all UK architectural schools are part of a university. Now, university schools have equal status within the profession but not within the educational establishment.

Syllabus

The syllabus of the RIBA exam includes design studies, materials, construction, structures, environmental design, building services, building economics, cultural context of building, and professional practice. The syllabus is included purely as a guide, as most students take their college exams. One of the most important features of architectural education is that it is based on a continuing series of design projects. Not only are these used to develop students' design skills; the technical skills which the student is learning can also be related to the design projects.

Practical training

Although the normal length of course is five years, it is possible to gain exemption from RIBA Part 2 after four years. A few colleges take advantage of this either by offering a four-year course or allowing you to do your final-year thesis for your college diploma on a more general subject than would be allowed by the RIBA. One of your two years of practical training can be taken before you complete Part 2 – normally between the third and fourth year – but the other year must always be taken after Part 2 (although some schools do not mind if you take additional years out during the course, it is just that you still have to do one year after Part 2).

Schools vary widely in the amount of help they give you in finding a job, although most confine their activities to maintaining a register of possible offices. However, others take a much more direct hand in the year out in order to ensure that students get particular experience, for example experience working for a contractor.

Other differences between courses

In addition to breaks in the college course for practical training, some colleges have a live projects office. Another way of getting a balance of school and practical training is the sandwich course. For example, the School of Architecture and Building Engineering at Bath University offers a six-year sandwich course (the same length as the standard five years' school and one year out), consisting of a cycle of 14 terms in the university interspersed with four terms in practical training. An increasing number of students decide to change school after Part 1, either because they find the school does not suit them or in order to broaden their experience.

You should also assess to what extent a course is design-based, whether it is very structured or allows you to follow your own inclination, or whether it is practically-oriented, arts-oriented, or very technological. The school's prospectus should provide a good answer to this. However, sooner or later you will want to visit the school, meet either the principal or registrar, and have a look round.

In many ways the best recommendation of a school are the students themselves. Architectural students are by nature very critical and you can soon find out by talking to them, and to recently qualified graduates, what their feelings are about their school. However, in the end the choice of a school is a personal one and, of course, dependent on being accepted.

To enter a school of architecture you will normally need at least two academic subjects at A-level, or one A- and two AS-levels. In addition you must have passed at least three other subjects at GCSE, two of which must be academic. Some schools will accept BTEC (or SCOTVEC) Certificates in Building Studies instead of A-levels, and for mature students work experience may also be taken into account. In Scotland you need a minimum of three passes at SCE Higher grade and two at Ordinary grade, four of which must be academic. A few schools insist on maths or a science at A-level, but most are flexible. Generally you can study the A-levels that interest you most, but you should have passed physics or chemistry, maths and English language at least at GCSE.

If full benefit is to be derived from an architectural course both arts and science subjects should be studied at sixth-form level. In some schools the mix of arts and science causes administrative difficulties in relation to the A-level examinations. If this is the case at your school, try to keep up with arts studies if there is only a 'science' sixth-form or vice versa if the emphasis in your school is on the arts. This dual approach forms a valuable foundation for architectural studies. It is helpful to compile a portfolio of freehand drawings which can be presented when you are called for interview at a school of architecture.

ARB has introduced its own list of school examinations it recognises for admission to the Register of Architects. You should therefore establish whether the course you intend to take is recognised both by RIBA and ARB.

List of architecture schools in the United Kingdom with courses recognised for exemption from the RIBA Examination in Architecture

★   Part-time course available for exemption from Part 2 only of the RIBA Examination.

★★   Exemption from Part 2 only of the RIBA Examination. Part 1 and the Professional Practice Examination to be completed elsewhere.

†   Part-time course available for exemption from Parts 1 and 2 of the RIBA Examination.

††   Exemption from Part I of the RIBA Examination only. Part 2 and the Professional Practice Examination to be completed elsewhere.

Aberdeen
Scott Sutherland School of Architecture, Robert Gordon University, Garthdee Road, Aberdeen AB9 2QB; 01224 263500

Bath
School of Architecture and Building Engineering, University of Bath, Claverton Down, Bath BA2 7AY; 01225 826826

Belfast
Department of Architecture and Planning, The Queen's University of Belfast, Belfast BT7 INN; 01232 245133

Birmingham
†Birmingham School of Architecture, Faculty of the Built Environment, University of Central England in Birmingham, Perry Barr, Birmingham B42 2SU; 0121 331 5130

Brighton
★School of Architecture and Interior Design, University of Brighton, Mithras House, Lewes Road, Brighton BN2 4AT; 01273 600900

Cambridge
University of Cambridge, Department of Architecture, 1 Scroope Terrace, Cambridge CB2 IPX; 01223 332950

Canterbury
Canterbury School of Architecture, Kent Institute of Art and Design, New Dover Road, Canterbury CT1 3AN; 01227 769371

Cardiff
The Welsh School of Architecture, University of Wales College of Cardiff, Bute Building, King Edward VII Avenue, Cardiff CF1 3AP; 01222 874438

Dundee
School of Architecture, Duncan of Jordanstone College of Art, University of Dundee, Perth Road, Dundee DD1 4HT; 01382 23261

Edinburgh
Department of Architecture, Heriot-Watt University, Edinburgh College of Art, Lauriston Place, Edinburgh EH3 9DF; 0131 221 6071

Department of Architecture, University of Edinburgh, 20 Chambers Street, Edinburgh EH1 1JZ; 0131 650 2306

Glasgow
Department of Architecture and Building Science, University of Strathclyde, 131 Rottenrow, Glasgow G4 0NG; 0141 552 4400 ext 3023

†The Mackintosh School, Department of Architecture, Glasgow University and Glasgow School of Art, 177 Renfrew Street, Glasgow G3 6RQ; 0141 353 4686

Huddersfield
Department of Architecture, School of Design Technology, University of Huddersfield, Queensgate, Huddersfield HD1 3DH; 01484 422288

Hull
†School of Architecture, Art and Design, University of Lincoln-

shire and Humberside, Strand Close, Kingston upon Hull HU2
9BT; 01482 440550

Leeds

†Leeds School of the Environment Architecture, Leeds Metropolitan University, Brunswick Terrace, Leeds LS2 8BU; 01132
832600 ext 4089

Leicester

†Department of Architecture, School of the Built Environment,
De Montfort University, The Gateway, Leicester LE1 9BH;
01162 577415

Liverpool

Liverpool School of Architecture and Building Engineering,
University of Liverpool, Abercromby Square, PO Box 147,
Liverpool L69 3BX; 0151 794 2604

★School of the Built Environment, Department of Architecture,
The Liverpool John Moore's University, Mount Pleasant Buildings, 98 Mount Pleasant, Liverpool L3 5UZ; 0151 231 3704

London

Architectural Association School of Architecture, 34–36 Bedford
Square, London WC1B 3ES; 0171 636 0974

Bartlett School, University College London, Wates House, 22
Gordon Street, London WC1H 0QB; 0171 387 7050

Department of Architecture, University of East London, Holbrook Centre, Holbrook Road, London E15 3EA; 0181 590 7722

School of Architecture and Landscape, University of Green-
wich, Oakfield Lane, Dartford, Kent DA1 2SZ; 0181 316 8000

School of Architecture, Kingston University, Knights Park,
Kingston upon Thames, Surrey KT1 2QJ; 0181 547 2000

Royal College of Art, Kensington Gore, London SW7 2EU; 0171
584 5020

Department of Architecture, South Bank University,
Wandsworth Road, London SW8 2JZ; 0171 928 8989

Department of Architecture and Interior Design, University of North London, 166–220 Holloway Road, London N7 8DB; 0171 753 5134

School of Architecture and Engineering, University of Westminster, 35 Marylebone Road, London NW1 5LS; 0171 911 5000

Manchester
Department of Architecture, Landscape and 3D-Design, The Manchester Metropolitan University, Loxford Tower, Lower Chatham Street, Manchester M15 6HA; 0161 247 1103

School of Architecture, University of Manchester, Manchester M13 9PL; 0161 275 6934

Newcastle
Department of Architecture, University of Newcastle, Newcastle upon Tyne NE1 7RU; 0191 222 6000

Nottingham
The Nottingham School of Architecture, Department of Architecture and Planning, University of Nottingham, University Park, Nottingham NG7 2RD; 0115 9513155

Oxford
School of Architecture, Oxford Brookes University, Gipsy Lane, Headington, Oxford OX3 0BP; 01865 483200

Plymouth
The Plymouth School of Architecture, University of Plymouth, The Hoe Centre, Notte Street, Plymouth PL1 2AR; 01752 233600

Portsmouth
School of Architecture, University of Portsmouth, King Henry I Street, Portsmouth POI 2DY; 01705 842083

Sheffield
School of Architectural Studies, University of Sheffield, Sheffield S10 2TN; 01142 768555

The RIBA Examination in Architecture and the Examination in Professional Practice

The recognised schools of architecture are exempted from the RIBA Examination and until recently the RIBA's own examination has mirrored the school pattern of examinations and project assessment, except that the Institute has required a single Comprehensive Design Project (CDP) for Parts 1 and 2.

The RIBA Examination provides a route for students specifically based in practice; for this reason the route through the examination has fewer written papers and more emphasis on project-based assessment, including project-related studies in the three main areas of supporting work which are called Technical, Professional and Cultural.

New entrants are required to have a minimum of six years' *certified* practical experience and entry requirements which are the equivalent of matriculation. The Examination Entry Committee makes a qualitative assessment of candidates who wish to enter for the examination and there is a limit placed on the numbers entering the commencement of the route to the examination each year. The examination is carefully structured; students are given an adviser and required to make tutorial arrangements for themselves. There is a minimum time of six years and a maximum of 14 years in which the four phases of the examination may be completed.

Entrants to Part 2, who have a school-based Part 1, are required to have three years of certified practical experience and have to satisfy the Entry Committee on the same qualitative basis as those entering for Part 1.

The Examination in Professional Practice, which all students who qualify by means of the RIBA Examination in Architecture have to take, requires candidates to produce a statement in support of their request to join the profession and evidence of their experience. No time limit is imposed but in most cases it is assumed that at least two years of experience as a post-Part 2 student will be necessary. The examination consists of two written papers and a professional interview. The standard set for the new examination is significantly more rigorous than the old.

There is no limit on the number of attempts a candidate may have at the Examination in Professional Practice.

The Examination in Architecture Part 1 and Part 2 is held in the Spring and new candidates applying to the Institute are given the relevant registration dates. The Examination in Professional Practice is held once each year in Spring. Details of all new examinations, together with current syllabuses and typical examination papers, may be obtained from the Examinations Office at the RIBA.

RIBA Practical Training Scheme

Objectives

Practical training is an essential complement to academic learning. The fundamental objectives of the Scheme are to ensure that, through 'learning by doing' with responsibility in a busy office, those entering the profession should have:

(a) a practical understanding of the legal, contractual and procedural aspects of professional architectural practice in the United Kingdom, which will be tested in the Part 3 examination;
(b) practical experience of obligations, both legal and ethical, arising from the relationships between architect and client and between employer and employee;
(c) direct experience, under supervision, of the duties and responsibilities of professional practice which become theirs on qualification.

Practical training must be recorded on an RIBA practical training record sheet. The record must be signed monthly by the supervising architect or the employer and it must be countersigned at approximately three-monthly intervals by the student's practical training adviser.

The minimum period of practical training is two years, all of which must be after the start of an architectural course and before sitting Part 3 of the RIBA Examination in Architecture (or the G3 examination where applicable) or the equivalent recognised examination in a school of architecture, and one of which must be after successfully sitting or gaining exemption from Part 2 of the RIBA Examination in Architecture.

Students normally take a year out, for example between the third year and fourth year, and work in an architect's office. Very short periods (less than three months) do not normally count.

A maximum of one year may be spent in research and development work provided this is the first year of practical training, the work is of a quality and nature to satisfy the objectives of the scheme, and it is supervised by a recognised specialist in the field.

A second year of practical training must be taken before taking Part 3 of the RIBA Examination in Architecture.

Useful addresses

Architects Registration Board, 73 Hallam Street, London W1N 5LQ; 0171 580 5861

British Institute of Architectural Technologists, 397 City Road, London EC1V 1NE; 0171 278 2206

British Standards Institution, 389 Chiswick High Road, London W4 4AL; 0181 996 9000

Building Research Establishment, Garston, Watford, Hertfordshire WD2 7JR; 01923 894040

Chartered Institution of Building Services Engineers, Delta House, 222 Balham High Road, London SW12 9BS; 0181 675 5211

Chartered Society of Designers, 29 Bedford Square, London WC1B 3EG; 0171 631 1510

Civic Trust, 17 Carlton House Terrace, London SW1Y 5AW; 0171 930 0914

Incorporated Society of Valuers and Auctioneers, 3 Cadogan Gate, London SW1X 0AS; 0171 235 2282

Institution of Structural Engineers, 11 Upper Belgrave Street, London SW1X 8BH; 0171 235 4535

Landscape Institute, 6 Barnard Mews, London SW11 1QU; 0171 738 9166

Royal Incorporation of Architects in Scotland, 15 Rutland Square, Edinburgh EH1 2BE; 0131 229 7205

Royal Institute of the Architects of Ireland, 8 Merrion Square, Dublin 2; 01 676 1703

Royal Institute of British Architects, 66 Portland Place, London W1N 4AD; 0171 580 5533

RIBA Eastern Region, 6 King's Parade, Cambridge CB2 1SJ; 01223 324157

RIBA East Midlands Region, 4 St James's Terrace, Nottingham NG1 6FW; 0115 941 3650

RIBA London Region, 66 Portland Place, London W1N 4AD; 0171 580 5533

RIBA Northern Region, Milburn House, Dean Street, Newcastle upon Tyne NE1 1LJ; 0191 232 4436

RIBA North West Region, 44–46 King Street, Knutsford, Cheshire WA16 6HJ; 01565 652 927

RIBA Southern Region, Massey's Folly, Church Road, Upper Farringdon, Alton, Hampshire GU34 3EG; 01420 587393

RIBA South East Region, 17 Upper Grosvenor Road, Tunbridge Wells, Kent TN1 2DU; 01892 515878

RIBA South Western Region, School of Architecture, University of Plymouth, Notte Street, Plymouth PL1 2AR; 01752 265921

RIBA Wales Region, Society of Architects in Wales, 75a Llandennis Road, Rhydypennau, Cardiff CF2 6EE; 01222 762215

RIBA Wessex Region, School of Architecture, University of Bath, Bath BA2 7AY; 01225 826649

RIBA West Midlands Region, Birmingham & Midlands Institute, Margaret Street, Birmingham B1 3SP; 0121 233 2321

RIBA Yorkshire Region, 8 Woodhouse Square, Leeds LS3 1AD; 0113 245 6250

Royal Institution of Chartered Surveyors, 12 Great George Street, Parliament Square, London SW1P 3AE; 0171 222 7000

Royal Society of Ulster Architects, 2 Mount Charles, Belfast BT7 1NZ; 01232 323760

Royal Town Planning Institute, 26 Portland Place, London W1N 4BE; 0171 636 9107

12 Further reading

A History of Architecture, Sir Banister Fletcher, 20th edition, edited by Dan Cruikshank, Oxford Architectural Press, 1996 (first published 1896).

Architecture, Form, Space and Order, F Ching, Van Nostrand Reinhold NY, 1979.

Experiencing Architecture, Steen Eiler Rasmussen, 2nd edition, MIT Press, 1962.

From Bauhaus to our House, T Wolfe, Cardinal Edition, Sphere Books, 1989.

Modern British Architecture, Jonathan Glancy, Thames and Hudson, 1989.

Skyscraper, The Making of a Building, Karl Sabbagh, Macmillan, 1989.

Sources of Modern Architecture and Design, Nikolaus Pevsner, 1968, Thames and Hudson, reprint 1975.

The Way We Build Now, Form, Scale and Technique, Andrew Orton, Van Nostrand Reinhold (UK), 1988.

Traditional Buildings of Britain, An Introduction to Vernacular Architecture, RW Brunskill, Victor Gollancz Ltd, 1989.

Your House. The Outside View, John Prizeman (foreword Richard Gloucester), a Blue Circle publication, Hutchinson and Co. Ltd, 1965.

Index

structural engineer   4, 9,
    40–41
surveyor   4, 39–40
syllabus   68–9

technician/technologist, *see*
    architectural
    technologist

tenders   9, 18
town planner   4, 41–2
trade unions   18

UNISON   18
university schools   68

year out   45–6

The Kogan Page *Careers in...* series